6 NECESSARY PROTECTIONS OF LIFE

EXPLORING UNCHARTED TERRITORIES OF LIFE

MANJUL MANISH

Contents

Preface   v

Prologue   vii

1. THEORY   1

2. Too Much Information   4

3. Success Is Overrated   16

4. Socialising In Isolation   23

5. Unnecessary Conversation   32

6. Unreal Love   41

7. Psychological Issues   48

8. Last !!!   59

Preface

A gathering place for ideas. Indeed, this was the initial impetus for me to write this book. We tend to over analyse things, waste time with meaningless chatter, and place too much stock on superficial relationships.

Within our ranks, we have discovered a new adversary " Distraction " . It's my goal to shield you from this kind of distraction .The ideas coalesced into words, and those words formed a theme. If you can find your own personal resonance with the book's central concept, it will enrich your life in profound ways.

Prologue

Bhagwat Gita says " Karmanye vadhikaraste Ma Phaleshu Kadachana,
Ma Karmaphalaheturbhurma Te Sangostvakarmani "

The literal meaning of this quote is , "You have the right to work only but never to its fruits.

Let not the fruits of action be your motive, nor let your attachment be to inaction"

It has a much deeper meaning.

Lord Krishna told Arjuna to fight in the manner of karma (self-righteousness) on the battlefield of Mahabharata, unattached to the fruit. Another facet of his devotion is his dislike of war. One will never reach the road of emancipation with such an attachment. Any kind of attachment, positive or harmful, may lead to bondage. Being silent is a sin. Thus, Arjuna could only find solace in fighting as a duty, unconcerned with the outcome.

Let me tell you a fact . If you get a chance to visit old Rajinder Nagar in Delhi , you will find thousands of UPSC aspirants . After momos the most common thing which you will notice is pamplets . Pamplets of coaching centres , study materials , books , notes and other academic stuff for students . In this pamplet somewhere in front or back it will written in Sanskrit" कर्मण्येवाधिकारस्ते मा फलेषु कदाचन।
मा कर्मफलहेतुर्भूर्मा ते सङ्गोऽस्त्वकर्मणि॥" (*Karmanye vadhikaraste Ma Phaleshu Kadachana,*
Ma Karmaphalaheturbhurma Te Sangostvakarmani)

"You should keep working without being worried about the result," reads the back page of the pamphlet, contradicting the front page's claim that "We are the best coaching institute in India and have the highest success percentage."

Perhaps this is the reason only 1 out of 10 students manage to clear UPSC in their first attempt . Because remaining ones just follow this quote and crack UPSC in 2nd , 3rd , 4th attempt or may be never . After all success rate in UPSC is around 0.2% .

I think this line should come with a disclaimer that while you must focus on your effort than the result , you should also have a failure strategy in mind . What if you don't succeed ? Failure is very common right .It's 99.8% . No ambitious person likes to hear the term "failure" because of how pejorative it is. How many ambitious people do you think would sign up for a motivating class whose title is "How to deal with failure"?

I think while preparing for any competetive exams you must have a failure strategy in mind . What if you fail ? That will make you more practical . In this strategy you must have a clear idea that how much effort you will put . How many attempts will you make .

A brilliant tactic in the stock market is the stop loss. This ensures that a loss of not more than 20 will be incurred if a stock purchased at 100 is sold. So, you'll be selling the stock the second its value drops below 80. Your stop loss should be 80. You are protected by 80. If you have decided that you will make 2 attempts , let these 2 attempts be your protection . And even if you miss this exam by half marks you will not try again .

This is the safeguard I'll be detailing for you in the book. You need that kind of protection. Because a strong defense is an even stronger defense if practiced right. In preparation for the many struggles you're sure to encounter, arm yourself with a shield.

CHAPTER ONE

THEORY

What's up?

"Protection"

When you first hear this word, what thoughts spring to your mind?

Well it could be anythng , but I think we can all agree on what comes to our mind first: India, with the dubious honour of being the world's most populated population it should have not only been in your thoughts but in your practice too . As opposed to being something you think about, it ought to be your top priority.

Can you think of any other probable explanation?

It can be Abdominal Guard if you're familiar with or play cricket. Depending on the weather, you may need a raincoat, a lock, an insurance policy, a helmet, a bulletproof vest, or even a bodyguard .

Physical safety is a common theme among them. We are aware of the precautions to take since it is crucial. However, are we aware of the measures that might safeguard us against psychological attacks, behavioural mentality, or any other abnormal pattern?

Even if we are aware of it, we still don't put it into practice since it doesn't matter to us. I shall discuss the necessary safeguards to defend ourselves from these mental attacks till the book is finished. If you implement these safeguards into your life, I guarantee you will feel that 24 hours seems like a much longer time than it does right now.

Let me go into details .

Protecting oneself against particular thoughts, behaviors, attitudes, or even habits is what I consider to be the definition of protection. In addition, I am not referring to behaviors such as picking one's nose, driving recklessly, smoking, drinking, stealing, or any other type of addiction. There are a variety of papers and films that are available everywhere, and there are plenty of them. I will explain the safeguards that I believe are necessary in order to alter my way of life and the actions that I have taken that have not only made me a more mature and better person, but also a better person overall.

This worry that it may be nothing more than my own personal sensation prompted me to get it cross-checked with a total of seventeen people who come from a variety of life styles and backgrounds, and they all came to the same conclusion. During the time that you could be reading this book, I will continue to engage in conversation with a greater number of individuals and look for affirmation themselves. I would like to request that you share your comments on social media by tagging me or using the hashtag #myprotectionoflife. Additionally, please let me know which of the several methods of life protection you have found to be helpful for you and that you might utilize in your daily routine.

To give you a taste of what's to come in this book, I'll tell you a small unfinished narrative. I want to make sure we stay on the same page.

A prisoner was condemned to fourteen years of severe incarceration. This prisoner was incarcerated. Accusations of murder were brought against him. In his statement, he claimed that he did it in self-defense; nevertheless, he did not have any proof to indicate that he was really innocent.He spent the whole time disciplining himself, making sure that he did not bother anybody, and avoiding becoming engaged in any kind of disturbance.

He remained one of the most honorable individuals that were incarcerated.By the time he had just a few days left in his release, he began to have feelings of anxiety. It was the last thing he wanted to do. Within the confines of the prison, life was pleasant; the warden was kind to him, and the other inmates held him in high regard. Despite the fact that there was a great deal of insanity, cruelty, and hard-core criminals, there was still a rule of law. Every single person exhibited mature behavior. On the other hand, the news from the outside was very awful. Absolutely no touch with the outside world was made by this prisoner. He was concerned about what he would do after he had emerged from the guardhouse. Carpentry work was required of him while he was incarcerated, and he was compensated for his work. The food was great as well.

Although everyone believed that being imprisoned is a failure, he believed that freedom would be a failure for him. When the final day arrived, he was anxious, he was unable to sleep, and he kept glancing out the window of his cell window. As well as just before the sun rose......

When the last chapter of this book is finished, this narrative will come to an end. Moreover, this book contains all that has been going through the thoughts of this prisoner.

Six different safeguards are essential for us to have in our day-to-day lives. Let's get started if you think you have what it takes to make the transaction of your life.

CHAPTER TWO

Too Much Information

How much information is enough ?

Your insatiable curiosity begs the question: why?For what reason are you interested in finding out which movie collections exist? If you were to pursue a degree in politics, what could you possible accomplish with it? Height of a notable personality. What is a cricketer's salary? Spouse of a politician. Please explain your plans for using this data. You may get the solution to any famous question on the Internet. "Why Gandhi did not saved Bhagat Singh ?" , "Is Gandhi responsible for partition of India ?" . "What are Nehru mistakes ?" "Did Savarkar wrote those mercy petitions ?" "What are the contentious verses in the Bible, the Quran, and the Gita?" Oh, and my personal favorite. Was Harmonium prohibited by Nehru?

Explain to me WHY... ?

WHY ...?

Why do you feel the need to know this information? Is there any way that this may radically alter your life? Are you simply trying to make a point in some part of the conversation? What is the reason behind your desire to appear knowledgeable and well-informed? Also, has it become into a habit for you?

Because it's possible that Sachin Tendulkar is unaware of the reason why Nehru banned Harmonium. To be honest, no one in the entire world will ever ask him that question. Nevertheless, he is well-known, renowned, and revered in the world. Your life will not be affected in any way by the fact that you do not know the reason why Nehru outlawed Harmonium.

When compared to the likelihood of someone asking you why Nehru banned Harmonium, the likelihood of you dying first is greater than 99.99 percent. There is a possibility that you will never require the information that you are looking for in your whole life. For that reason, it is completely unneeded.

And this is not the end of the story; as soon as "Lord Internet" notices that you are looking for Nehru and Harmonium, it will begin providing you with information on other musical instruments. For example, you may receive a recommendation to purchase a flute and a tabla at a low cost. Spending ten to fifteen minutes on YouTube listening to music that is relaxing is a possibility. If you listen to this calm soundtrack, you could find yourself watching strange climbing videos. If you continue watching these films, you will be taken to Sadhguru, who will discuss the significance of mountains in our lives. The incredible life-altering statements that Sadhguru has to offer will be shared further. Now, as soon as you open the channel of spirituality, YouTube will begin to bombard you with videos featuring Gaur

Gopal Das, Sri Sri Ravi Shankar, and other well-known holy gurus.

Once you reach that location, there is a high probability that you will come across a video that will make fun of spirituality. You continue to watch this for two more minutes, and footage of stand-up comedians will begin to appear on the screen. A few of them will make fun of current politicians, some of whom you might or might not find particularly appealing. You are going to leave a remark on this video regardless of the outcome. It is because of this that YouTube will offer to you a video in which a television journalist is out in the field talking to random people about the same stand-up comic or this politician that the comedian was roasting, and one of the guys will ask, "Do you know that Indira Gandhi killed Rajiv Gandhi?"

Then, without even recognizing that Rajiv Gandhi passed away after Indira Gandhi, you would instantly be searching the internet for information on this. Believe me when I say that this is one of the queries that gets searched for the most on Google.

So, allow me to ask you once more. Why do you require such a broad range of information?

The correct response is that you do not, and even if you do require any knowledge, it is not essential that you remember it; thus, therefore - please refrain from remembering random information. When you notice that the random person is merely spouting passages from a holy book, it puts a lot of pressure on you to seem intelligent and informed. I know that this is something that gets you excited on a regular basis. In addition, you should begin by searching for material on Google and then begin to commit it to memory.

It is not required, my dear, It is not required at all. I hope that being well-informed becomes a regular practice in schools as well. In any case, children will be able to recall the periodic table.

There is no problem with this information. It is still possible to digest it, and most importantly, it is a product of your nation. The first five options that come up when you search "why America," are invasions of Iraq, Japan, Israel, Vietnam, and a number of other countries. The list continues on.

If you were to imagine yourself seated next to the President of the United States, what would be the first question you would ask?

How are you doing today?

It's possible that an engineer may inquire about your salary.

It's possible that a politician will inquire about how to obtain a ticket for your party.

Wouldn't it be reasonable for a journalist to inquire about the policies of the country?

However, the question of why you invaded these countries will not be asked by anyone other than a terrorist.

Even more crucial, no one will inquire about this matter towards you. Are you aware of the reasons why the United States invaded? Even during the interview for the UPSC?

It is not necessary for you to be aware of this.

Whether you believe this is odd or not, the reality that between the years 2015 and 2017 , an enormous number of individuals looked into the reasons for Katappa's murder of Bahubali. Please type "why Amitabh," and the first idea is to ask why Amitabh chose to marry Jaya.

As you could have guessed, even Mr. Bachhan himself will not ask you this question on his show on the KBC.

The need for speculation is very high. How come the stock market is going down? Among the stocks, which one has the largest dividend? Where can I find the finest stock to invest in at the moment? What is more advantageous, a stock or a mutual fund?

However, the truth is that fewer than ten percent of individuals participate in the Indian stock market, despite the fact that the number of people who ask these concerns is far greater. These queries are not entirely without merit. It indicates that there are a great number of people who are just interested in information, in the same way. They are not going to take any action based on this information.

Up until this point, I have been discussing stuff that has at least occurred in the same universe. There are a lot of individuals who are inquisitive about whether or not there is life beyond the planet.

I feel sorry for NASA and ISRO. In order to obtain information that can be readily looked for by a random individual on Google, they are investing billions and billions of dollars.

The Internet is odd, but the actual conversation is much stranger than the Internet itself.

What percentage of the time do you hear people talking about the romance between Malaika Arora and Arjun Kapoor? The fact that people are verifying their age difference is the most idiotic thing that can happen. Well, that is gossip, and it will continue to happen. What plans do you have for utilizing this information?

Create new guidelines for marriage?

Being well-informed can sometimes put one in a precarious position.

During live discussions, I have witnessed certain individuals searching for information. When a politician asked another politician who the agricultural minister is during one of the television discussions on the farm bill, the other politician had to actually google the answer after being asked the question. A piece of knowledge that is required, but can you predict what we Indians did throughout that phase?

We looked at whether or not farm bills are beneficial. We are interested in the analysis of the information more than we are in the information itself. Even in the most extreme endeavour to acquire knowledge, we are not seeking for the information in its original form.

This insatiable desire for knowledge is something that information suppliers are obviously aware of. It is not surprising that we have more than 400 news outlets; when you take into account print media, independent journalists, YouTubers, bloggers, random people on Twitter, and, most importantly, whatsapp forwards, you are literally presented with a variety of information on a platter.

More than what is necessary, more than what your digestive system is able to process. When I was looking for information regarding a certain verse from a religious literature, I came across some. It was a pretty lengthy conversation over Whatsapp. Throughout the entirety of the conversation, it was discussed that this passage states that a man is authorised to beat his wife. The document included a number of examples and several events that had occurred in India, all of which were articulated with dates and the location where they took place. In it, there were substantial descriptions of a few practices that were linked.

Information was provided to me by it. Having said that, I made the effort to read the full article, despite the fact that I was concerned about the possibility of receiving incorrect information. I also double verified it, and I discovered that it was accurate, if not in a literal sense. What I was unable to comprehend was the question of what is to be done with this information. Okay, I believe that every religion has certain traditions that aren't proper, and others are speaking out against them as well. I, like every other person, have been reading more about it. I consulted a great deal of material that was readily available on the internet and then formed my own conclusion. However, I will say it again: what am I going to do with this opinion? In full seriousness, I have rehearsed a speech on the subject. I am preparing my response in my thoughts while I am sitting in my bathroom, listening to the call of nature. I am only waiting for someone to claim that "Every religion practices gender equality," and then I will begin, I will begin the conversation with my collection of knowledge. I am just waiting for someone to say that. I will present it in such a way that everyone around me will be unable to comprehend what I am saying. What if I were to be given the opportunity to deliver a speech on this subject on a stage? There will be YouTubers who will utilize my speech to create videos, shorts, and insta reels, and the audience will be completely taken aback by it themselves. I am going to be famous and I am going to be everywhere.

Unfortunately, no one has ever told me this in front of me, despite the fact that it is a wonderful dream. As a matter of fact, I have begun following a large number of people on social media who frequently express themselves in this manner. In this regard, even they have not made any statements.

The situation is not just. Despite the fact that I have sharpened my instruments, nobody is fighting. Now all that is required of me is to initiate this Vietnam War; I need to establish a foundation for such a conversation, so that individuals will speak out and talk about this subject, and I will be there to provide a middle ground.

The issue with receiving information that is not essential is that. I was never in need of it. In spite of this, I took it, committed it to memory, and made it a point to ensure that in the event that there are situations in which the subject matter is similar to this, I would quickly step in with this knowledge. The only reason for this is because I am well-informed.

I have learned how to drive in a city where there were no automobiles. What should I do now ? Learn how to construct automobiles?

When you are looking for information, you run the risk of entering a potentially hazardous region, which is disinformation. This item is presented to you in a package, a packaging that is so exquisitely created that it will take you on a ride.

Let me illustrate this with an example. Assume that you have a strong dislike for a politician, and in order to maintain your level of knowledge, you look for errors committed by that person. It has now been heard by the internet. After this, some magic will take place that is powered by artificial intelligence, and you will begin to get forwards on WhatsApp that discuss this politician. There will be a random forward that has a detailed itinerary of how this politician travelled to a different country and spent some time at a relaxation center. One of the staff members was killed as a result of a quarrel that he had with the proprietor of the spa. This will be followed by a photo of that minister inside a spa (you will not bother to check if it is indeed a spa), and then there will be a news piece reporting the unexplained disappearance of a staff member in some spa, and then your confirmation bias will lead you to trust an article that confirms this information.

There is no doubt that you will accept this. It is the packaging, which consists of a sandwich of information that is both accurate and deceptive, interspersed with a collection of news items. It is something that everyone with an average intelligence level will believe. I don't need to tell you what the average intelligence level of our country is. (Don't google it, just leave it be)

Do you remember the history lessons you took in school or the general knowledge ones you took?

The date of Babar's invasion of India, the length of time that the Panipat Battle lasted, the date of birth of "a random political figure," and the author of the well-known book "some random motivational book" are all questions that need solving.

What in the world am I going to do with this information when it comes to me?

It has come to my attention that there are several online schools available in our culture that instruct their students in nursery rhymes. With rhymes as perplexing as this one

Three Blind Mice , Three Blind Mice

See how they run , see how they run

The first question is why you feel the need to repeat it. Whether you are instructing a youngster or a person with mental retardation, or whether you have the same method to deal with both of them, what is the difference?

In any case...

This continues to be the case.

They all run after the farmer's wife

She cut off their tails with a carving knife (*that's gory*)

Did you ever see such a sight in your life as three blind mice

Would you think that a child who is between the ages of five and six is made to repeat this statement a staggering number of times? He is unaware of the significance of these words; in fact, I have never seen a blind mouse in my whole life, and I am unsure as to whether or not a mouse genuinely experiences these conditions, such as blindness, baldness, obesity, jealousy, or maybe even constipation. But this is the content that children are being taught in school. I am aware that your hand is slowly reaching for your mobile in order to determine whether or not a mouse may be blind.

Kindly refrain from doing that. It is not necessary for you to have this information at all. In the event that you are truly unable to control yourself, you should look for this music on YouTube.

Did you pay attention?

From this point on, this rhyme will get ingrained in your mind, and you will continue to rhyme it for the remainder of the day until you come across anything that is even more irritating.

That's the key to success.

It has been demonstrated that humming is an effective method for relieving tension. It is beneficial to your health. It enables you to freely express feelings that you have been repressing.

In a way, I agree with you, but I'm concerned about the impact it has on others around you. The consequences that it has for the individual who continues to rhyme it for a number of days or weeks. Sometimes a song will manage to become stuck in your mind, and it's quite normal. It prevents you from thinking and from concentrating on anything.

When you want to be joyful, you need to let yourself get lost in a notion. Oh, that's exactly the idea. The theory is sound. But the point I'm trying to make is that you may allow a youngster to get lost in their own thoughts just by letting them play.

And if you believe that education is equally essential, then you should teach him how to correctly wash his hands, tie his shoelaces, learn the names of his city, his residence address, and the information about his parents. Even if he gets lost, he might at least be able to tell you where he is.

I don't want to be in a situation when a youngster is missing and when he is queried about his location, he sings "three blind mice" in a loud voice.

In no way am I suggesting that being well-informed is not a positive thing. Let me illustrate this with an example. Assume that you are on a trip and that you decide to go to Hampi, which is a fantastic location in the state of Karnataka. You already have your belongings packed and are getting ready to go. What are some of the things that you would like to be informed about?

Hampi is located where?

What is the distance between the nearest airport and the nearest train station?

Are there any ways to get to Hampi?

Activities available in Hampi

Locations to stay in

The best restaurants that are currently accessible

Locations where one may go shopping

Historic sites and places

The weather

Do you concur? Okay, go obtain this information; it will be helpful; however, why do you watch a video blog about traveling to Hampi? The movie is twenty-two minutes long and has a woman talking about herself, her car, and the personnel at her hotel, as well as making strange faces while munching on some bizarre cuisine from some random places. Within a film that is 22 minutes long, there will be a video of the real place that is less than two minutes long, and even that information is not required.

There is no reason for you, buddy, to adopt your mind to feel the same way that that foolish YouTuber is feeling. You are going to travel to that location, and you are going to experience it for yourself.

Your experience will be ruined as a result.

You are required to have your own personal experience. My personal preference is for mountains over beaches, and this is something that I have experienced. The manner in which a vlogger communicates this, as well as their thoughts on the matter, are irrelevant to me.

I have a suggestion: create a video blog about the creepy and terrifying scary rooms that you can discover at shopping malls, and then publish it to YouTube. As a matter of fact, if it makes its way to the administrator of the shopping center, he will file a lawsuit against you since you have removed the element of surprise from the scenario, much like a movie spoiler.

A tourist destination can be spoiled by a video blog. You are not required to have this information.

The same is true for food youtube channels. Hunger is, in my opinion, both the greatest blessing and the worst curse that God has bestowed upon us. When you have the ability to provide for your own needs, it is a blessing; nevertheless, when you do not have the financial means to do so, it is a misfortune.

In the event that you have more than a million other ways to spend your money, the fact that someone is spending money to purchase this book indicates that you have the funds to provide for yourself, or at the very least, that you have someone who can make it happen for you. To get a better sense of the flavor, you should eat it rather than watch it. In the same way that every human person has their own unique fingerprint, every human being also has their own tongue print. Something may taste delicious to someone else, but it may not taste the same to you. To put that into perspective, that is how diverse God has formed us, and yet you put your faith in a random YouTuber for his views.

Therefore, it is beneficial to get this information about the establishments that provide the greatest kebab; nevertheless, it is a waste of time to stroll about and watch random videos of individuals and observe their reactions after eating each and every piece of kebab. It is not necessary.

In spite of the fact that songs, movies, books, and podcasts are all wonderful things, the question is whether you are utilizing them for the purpose of gaining knowledge or experience. Believe me when I say that if you take pleasure in them, you are almost certainly more knowledgeable than the individual who is approaching this as if it were a textbook. You need to enjoy what you are consuming.

Your internet speed and the amount of time you have available are some factors that might affect the flow of information.

In the past, when individuals had a lot of spare time, the internet was slow. However, in the modern age, where time isn't as readily available, the speed of the internet solves every problem. Consider the life of a person who is able to access high-speed internet in addition to having a lot of free time. An example of this would be a man who is now without a job and is still seeking for competitive tests, or a bachelor who is working hard to impress his coworkers and is searching the internet for fresh ideas to do this. The topic of how to make a girl feel special is one of the most sought topics on the internet. Would you be able to execute that even if you were to discover the specifics on how to wow someone?

Put this book down, go look at yourself in the mirror, and then come back before you continue reading.

Just what did you observe? Did you feel let down?

Now look at her pictures.

Just what did you observe? Is there hope?

Make an effort to comprehend this temporal order. Disappointment comes first, followed by hope.

I am about to share with you a remarkable fact, and I do it with a sad heart. There is also material on the internet on how to pass the UPSC or IIT exam; nevertheless, less than one percent of people really pass it. Despite the fact that the internet provides knowledge on how to win the World Cup, only one nation out of a total of twelve wins it.

The knowledge itself is not the important thing; what matters is what you do with the information. It is possible that you will provide me with more ways to get wealthy than the internet itself if I ask you how to become wealthy; but, do you follow it?

If you have the time and the internet bandwidth, you should focus on acquiring a skill rather than knowledge. This, however, is not the conclusion of the story. If you want to learn how to drive, you will not be able to do it just over the internet; you will need to actually drive yourself in order to acquire the necessary skills. It is not for you that the speed of the internet has been increasing day by day. However, for the researchers working for NASA and ISRO. Waiting patiently for your movie to load is something you can do.

In no way am I suggesting that the act of obtaining knowledge is not beneficial. Could you please tell me who does not collect information? For everyone. When it comes to running our everyday lives, we all require some knowledge. It is necessary for us to have a great deal of knowledge in order to travel to a location that we have never been before. In the past, we obtained this information from a random person on the street, but now we receive it from Lord Google. Do you have somebody who does not require information?

Someone who is alone in his or her world, who does not engage in social interaction, who does not communicate or share his life with other people, and who does not require any information is referred to as a lonely guy. It makes no difference to him why Israel and Palestine are fighting, why Russia attacked Ukraine, who will win the next elections, or what India's prospects are of winning the cricket world cup in 2023. He can't care less about any of these things.

The day that he lives, or rather the day that he survives, is over. Will you be able to guess the reason?

Now, he does not have to demonstrate his abilities to anyone. The things that he already knows are sufficient for him. You can be spoiled by money earned more than what you are able to spend, together with intellect, time, love, and information. You can also be spoiled by information.

It is not essential to move heaven and earth in order to acquire information in order to appear intelligent. However, it is important to avoid being misinformed and ill-informed. Trust me when I say that it is not worth it; it is simply not worth it.

If you want to watch a movie that you really, really want to watch, you should avoid watching the trailer because you will have a better time watching the movie.

In addition to this, I am unable to agree with anything else.

CHAPTER THREE

Success is Overrated

The author, Doctor Desmond Morris, said in his book titled "The Cat World" that out of twenty hunts that a tiger goes on, they only have one successful pursuit. 5%, to be exact.

It has a success ratio of 5%. If we flip this over and look at it from the perspective of a prey, we find that their success rate is 95%. This indicates that if you are being pursued by a tiger, there is a 95% probability that you will survive.

It is said that the failure of one individual is the success of another. Therefore, this is the ultimate truth.What are the levers of success? This is the same paradigm of success that you will find in the workplace, in the classroom, in the corporate world, and in sports. At every turn, individuals are engaging in competition with one another and establishing new benchmarks of achievement.

On the other hand, there is a group of individuals who are not competitive in any way. They go about their daily lives as if they are only surviving; it is possible that they are not even living their lives. In spite of this, there is still a sense of accomplishment. Each and every day that you have lived is a success. This sensation was shared by all of us throughout the COVID epidemic. When you were not impacted by Covid, did you not find it to be a satisfying feeling?

On the other hand, in the end, it happened to everyone. After we were affected, what emotions did we experience? It did not provide any difficulties at all. Consequently, the influence of success was lost. It only lasted for a very little period of time.

If you want to know what it's like to be the best in any class, ask Australia after they won the world cup. Inquire of Messi after he has scored a goal. How much longer does the sensation of triumph last? An individual who was a student at IIT was sentenced to jail for sexual assault, and you can probably imagine what many engineering students have scrawled on their walls: "Success is IIT" or maybe something else.

That you have not spent a significant amount of time viewing videos on how to be successful or that you have not mentally made some attempt to be successful in everything that you have encountered is not something that you should be telling me. Attempts to achieve the highest possible grade in the class, to triumph in a race or a music competition, to secure a job that pays well, and to make a good impression on the female of your choice. If you are able to get a yes as a reaction to an effort that you have made in a public area while kneeling down with an expensive diamond ring, then you have achieved success.*(in your head)*

On the other hand, what if she declines? Is it going to be a loss, a failure, or would it just be a rejection?

On the other hand, if you have been married for a number of years and you have a particularly unpleasant argument with your spouse, you are extremely likely to have the following feeling: "Was that Yes a success or a trap, a delusion?"

Acquiring wealth is, without a doubt, a measure of success for many people. Is there a measurement of just how much wealth is enough

I have asked a lot of individuals, and the majority of them have said that they want to be wealthy enough to live a respectable lifestyle.

Once more, what constitutes a respectable lifestyle?

I have witnessed that people who work in jobs that pay them just enough to get by each day are considerably happy than many millionaires. Is contentment synonymous with success?

However, a person may experience happiness for a little period of time, such as while they are inside dyeing, when they see their family sleeping on the floor, or when they watch their friends having a luxurious lifestyle.

However, success may be measured in comparison. Nevertheless, it is a highly erroneous assumption; it is impossible to be superior to anybody else in this world in each and every facet of life. This is due to the fact that there are some processes that cannot be reversed in this world. It is possible for you to lose your hair, and this is not going to change. You will grow older, and you will not be able to become younger.

There is a certain amount of competitiveness that you are destined to lose.

In the world of success, there is no pattern. An aspirant to the field of engineering who is very talented and clever might not pass an examination, yet a student who is mediocre might pass. The phrase "attitude" is used by some, while others would use "luck." It's possible that success is about attitude, but it might also be about chance.

Luck alone, without any capabilities, without any effort, and without any discipline. Success is nothing more than a matter of luck, and every single motivational speaker ought to resign their profession.

Even if you achieve success that is well-deserved and all of your dreams come true one by one, you get a decent job that pays you a salary that is higher than any of your friends, you get married to a beautiful girl who can give tough competition to any Bollywood celebrity, you live in a well-structured bungalow, and you enjoy respect in both your personal and professional life, you still have a lot of things to be thankful for. And then, on a certain day, when you get up out of bed right after supper, you discover that you are experiencing discomfort in your back. Because of how bad it is, you are unable to stand up properly and must instead sit on the ground. The anxious wife of yours rushes to you in a hurry, but she is unable to provide much assistance. It is unclear to her whether she should call for assistance or take you to the doctor. She is in a condition of dual consciousness. Given your weight, it is possible that she will not be able to lift you. She does not have any experience behind the wheel, and the waiting period for a taxi is ten minutes. Furthermore, it is not certain that the taxi driver will arrive or cancel at the very last minute.

A fascinating tale, wouldn't you agree?

If you think it is strange, let me tell you that approximately ten crore people in India are suffering from severe back pain, that less than seven percent of women know how to drive, and that you are already aware of the problem of passengers waiting for taxis and having their reservations cancelled.

The first thing the doctor says to him when he arrives at the hospital is that the sitting posture of today's working class is a significant concern. They should prioritize their health and take breaks at regular intervals. And at this very moment, just at this very moment, it will be difficult for that individual to evaluate the level of achievement he has achieved.

It would not be worth it to achieve success if it came at this price. And by the way, why is it necessary for us to refer to this as a success? When it comes to me, success is salvation. At the point that you are able to rise beyond the sensation of want and handle all feelings in the same manner, you have reached the stage where you are successful. But that is what I believe, and it's possible that you don't share my opinion. To you, success can mean being able to afford a fancy automobile or being completely debt-free.

If you have ever driven a Mercedes, you should know that driving a Maruti is not as easy as driving a Mercedes. It is not that you are unable to drive; rather, it is that you are confined inside the confines of success and that confinement will not permit you to drive a Maruti. Taking Shahrukh Khan as an example, his success does not let him to enjoy the bhelpuri when he is on the road. Despite the fact that he would claim that he does not desire that and that he is content with his status, he is unable to obtain it even if he were to desire it. As far as I can tell, that is the most extreme type of slavery.

You are employed at an office, right? It is not a novel notion; every individual who belongs to the working class has conceived of some kind of business at some point in their lives; nevertheless, the question is whether or not you are able to put it into action. This is what happens when you achieve success; it diminishes your ability to think creatively or think critically.

When it comes to slavery, there is no more egregious form than prosperity.

Post-success syndrome is a well-known condition that people experience. The effects of this sickness have been more severe than those of post-traumatic syndrome, in my experience. One possible explanation is that Trauma, in any case, has fangs, but Success has those adorable paws that you want to kiss every time you see them. The taste of success is delicious. It provides a pleasant sensation, although it has a very short hangover duration. The feeling of drunkenness does not last for very long.

When the sensation of achievement is no longer present, you have a sense of being a failure, someone to whom no one gives value. You have fond memories of your birthdays when you were younger. If you did not have a difficult childhood, I am confident that you would have cherished your birthday. But make an effort to recall the day following that. What do you recall the sensation being? a state of mind in which you do not feel unique or exceptional, but rather in which you feel like you are simply another person.

After achieving achievement, the situation remains the same.

Jim Carrey once stated, "I wish everyone could experience being rich and famous so that they would see that this is not an answer to anything."

Jim Carrey was referring to this same fact I am trying to explain. I have just read this on whatsapp, so I am not sure if he truly said that or not. However, I must say that it is an excellent remark.

To get to the point, however, I would want to know what you consider to be a successful marriage.

A marriage that stays together for more than half a century?

Alternatively, what about a marriage that only lasts for ten years but is filled with love and significance, and then when things didn't work out the pair decides to end it .

Or a marriage in which one of the partners has entirely surrendered in front of the other, in order for this marriage to be successful?

You will not be able to discover, nor will you be able to comprehend. In other words, it is the point. Success is a matter of opinion and is based on perception.

It may be a competition, it could be luck, it could be satisfaction, it could be wealth, or it could be something else entirely. Any thing might be the case.

That is not the message that is being spread in this contemporary environment. Not in accordance with what a number of wealthy YouTubers and authors claim about it.

Whether you're looking for ten suggestions to be successful, or how to be successful in life, or how to attain success in one hundred days, these youtube channels and books will convince you that success is the pinnacle of all accomplishments. You get accepted into the IIT, and you have achieved . You have successfully entered AIIMS that's it and when you are rich , that's an ultimate achievement .

Yes, achieving financial success is true. All of the items you have are branded. But is that going to be the end of it?

Regardless of the explanations I have attempted to provide, it will be hard for you to comprehend if you consider success to be the pinnacle of accomplishment. You must realize that, just like satisfaction, success is a state of mind.

Permit me to illustrate this with my own life. I am able to afford almost anything that I require.to live my life. Never in my life will I be able to afford to drive a premium vehicle. The reason I write is because I just enjoy writing, and even if there are only a few people who buy my work, I am fine with it. As soon as people who have read the book provide positive feedback, I will consider my work to have been successful.

Now, let's imagine that one of my books is successful, and let's say that this book becomes viral, as we say in this day and age, and that makes the sales skyrocket. I end up becoming a best-selling book author, I start giving interviews, I talk about my book, I become famous, I have all of my social media handles verified, people talk about me, a random YouTuber recommends my book, and some pieces of my book are featured in viral YouTube shorts and Instagram reels. All of these things happen because the book store is constantly demanding more copies from publications.

I anticipate that my conception of success will shift at this point. To me, this is a successful outcome.

If I produce one more book after this one and it does not meet the same destiny as this one, I will be quite dissatisfied. This is because my conception of success has shifted, and now I evaluate my success based on the number of volumes that I have sold rather than on the number of favorable reviews that I have received. Despite the fact that you spew trash about my book, you should still buy it. Isn't that extremely practical, but is that my genuine character, or does the goal post of success constantly shifting? Who knows?

This is success; it will entice you, it will perplex you, it may even corrupt you, it will not necessarily fulfill your needs, and it is often overrated.

When there are three trimesters in a year, where there are sixty students in a school, more than ninety percent of the pupils have a possibility of achieving a rank between one and three in the past ten years. At one moment or another, everyone of them achieved a level of success in their respective classes. What are your thoughts when you observe so many successful people congregating together?Being successful is so easy and common , isn't it .

More over thirty percent of the population of Afghanistan is illiterate, making it one of the most illiterate countries in the world. Literacy is a key factor in success in Afghanistan.

Do you genuinely believe this? Over one hundred and twenty-five countries have a literacy rate that is greater than ninety percent. In their opinion, the achievement of success in terms of literacy in Afghanistan is grossly exaggerated.

Whenever you begin the process of accomplishing something, whether it be obtaining a degree or passing an admission exam, impressing someone, preparing something, learning how to play a musical instrument, becoming pregnant, obtaining a job, learning how to drive, swimming, sword fighting, cricket, football, or anything else, you are making progress. In the event that you are intent on achieving achievement, you will only be concerned with the outcome, and not with the method itself. I repeat this statement because it is true.

During the process, you will never be able to fully appreciate and experience each and every moment. It is similar to mathematics in that you could obtain the correct answer, but you are unsure of how you got there. In the experiment known as Bernauli's trial, if any event can only have two outcomes, then the likelihood of one of those outcomes is only fifty percent. That certainly makes sense, doesn't it? Are you going to flip a coin and find out what the odds are of obtaining heads? 50 percent

You should know that when you invest in a company, there is a fifty percent possibility that it will rise up, but the success ratio of the stock is only ten percent. This is due to the fact that when someone bought in the stock, they just saw the outcome, and they did not see how they acquired it.

That is not only an overstated success, but it is also deadly due to the fact that it is unintentional. In addition to destroying you, it will make your life a living hell. In the event that you are truly interested in acquiring knowledge, you should not be thinking about achieving accomplishment. It is just okay, not like what I thought it would be, not bad definitely, but not that great, you know what, with so much buzz going around this, the entire world talks about this, everyone craves about this, it is overhyped, it is overrated, and it is overrated. If you enjoy the journey, you will definitely arrive at the destination, and then you will say, along with me, that the journey was much better, extremely satisfying, and unforgettable. And this is the future, the result that we call success.

CHAPTER FOUR

Socialising in Isolation

In order to finish the book, which is about avoiding distractions, I need to know how to do it without mentioning social media.

As I like to refer to it, social media is like a delicious snake that is only as dangerous as you want it to be. Any time you go near to it, it will become even closer. When you realize that you are getting deeper into its web, you realize that it is all around you, and it has seized you in such a manner that you cannot come out of it. It will play with you, conceal its fangs, and show you an image that you want to see. It will not bite you because if it did, it would be pretty obvious. It will play with you. You have to take a look at what it displays, consume what it offers, and pay attention to what it offers. You are being manipulated by it. It has only received the information it needed from your first few searches; its algorithm will handle the rest.

Although your oxygen supply is decreasing, you will not be suffocating as a result of this. For a frog that is being tossed into hot water, it operates in precisely the same manner as it does for all other animals. When it is dumped into ordinary water and then the water is gradually heated, the frog does not detect that it has been thrown outdoors or that the water has been heated. It is already too late for the frog to grasp what is happening. Heat claims the life of the frog.

There is the same phenomenon that occurs with us. The typical Indian spends more than 2:30 hours every day on various social media platforms. Do you believe that we are aware of that?

In no way. We do not do this unless we notice the clock and think, "Gosh, it's six o'clock in the evening or eight o'clock in the morning." If I do this, I will be late to the workplace because the instant I open my eyes, my hands immediately go out to my mobile device, and the first thing I see is Instagram or Facebook.

WHY is that?

If your response is simply to check in casually or to anticipate receiving a message, then I am sad to say that you are incorrect. We are no longer concerned about it.You are interested in finding out WHY ? If you remove the social media app that you use the most on your mobile device for just one day, you will notice that you are checking your mobile device more than ten times a day in search of the same app.

However, you have not removed the application in your mind. Your mind is still preoccupied with it, and you are searching for it in your portable device. Because you have made using your social networking app a habit, it is the first thing that you see when you open your device.

I'm sure the majority of you will agree with me on this, but could you perhaps explain why you've made it a habit?

One of the most important reasons is because it is always experiencing change. There is a higher volatility in your social media profile than that of the stock market. Yes, it is true .If you had made an investment in the Kospi Index Japan over the past thirteen years, you would have received a return of little more than two percent throughout that time period.

I present an example that is not only philosophical but rather based on concrete realities.

In other words, your social media page is characterized by its spontaneous nature. The question is, however, why does it vary each time?This is due to the fact that the number of people you follow on social media continues to add something new every time.

If you do not follow anybody on social media, your page will not have any updates, and you will likely spend less time on it.

Nevertheless, that is not going to take place.

There is a threesome going on between celebrities, social media platforms, and major brands. , They are now engaged in a conversation, having a good time and making money at the same time. In reality, we are just wasting our time and, in some cases, our money, even though we truly believe that we are having a good time.

Sometimes we don't pick up our phones to check social media simply because we have a habit of doing so. Other times, it's because a single individual who is really active on social media continues calling me on her page. It is the incessant desire that we have within our heads to go to her page and check out the most recent update. It would be possible to see where she traveled if she had shared the fresh picture that she had taken for the new reel.

When compared to the previous scenario, this one is much more ridiculous. In this situation, you are still not functioning like a computer, but rather like a foolish human person whose brain is keeping a significant portion of its capacity busy contemplating her. It is most likely that she is unaware of you, but with the help of her prior postings, she has gained an understanding of the kind of posts that receive the most likes and views. Isn't that the only thing that really matters?

This is something that the platform is also aware of, and it is the reason why your interest in social media is growing just because you have a few individuals who you like. The only reason they pay people is to keep people blogging, and they also pay individuals according on how engaged they are on social media.

This is the point at which the game is being played.

But believe me when I say that none of these are the primary reasons why you have a social media account or why you check in to social media every day or maybe every few hours and spend hours and hours on it.

Isolated socialization is the explanation for this occurrence. In the event that you did not get this, allow me to expound about it in further detail.

In the first place, let's look at each of these terms on their own.

Socializing entails engaging in conversation with individuals, integrating oneself into society, acquiring new acquaintances, and establishing a network of contacts.

To be isolated implies to be alone and to avoid interacting with other people.

When you are socializing in isolation, you want to see other people, you want to know their responses, how they talk, how they behave, what they are doing, their current life partners, their choice of clothes, items they buy, places they visit, and food they eat. You also want to know what they are doing.

Instead of stopping there, you continue to watch their vlogs and the photographs that they have tagged. This is not something that only applies to a celebrity; it is also possible for this to occur with your neighbour since you are familiar with both their name and their face. This is the start of a dangerous game . Following this, you begin searching for him on social media, and when you do locate him, the next step is to begin the game of interacting with him. There are instances when the profile is blocked, which is unfortunate, but for the most of the time, you are responsible for finding your new buddy on social media.

You are aware that there have been several instances in which two individuals are connected on social media, but they never communicate to each other in person, even if they meet in person. Taking the game of socializing to a greater level is what you are doing here."

It is very evident that social media is not about interacting with others; rather, it is solely about violating the privacy of individuals. A type of seclusion that a person feels comfortable sharing with others.

While participating in the discussion program Koffee with Karan, a Bollywood actor once stated that there are instances when we don't even know that we have spoken a lot about ourselves in public. This statement was made during an interview about the show.

When someone posts pictures, comments, or videos on social media, they are actually revealing more than they would like to do. This is something that happens every single day. Simply put, it occurs all of a sudden.

And then there are even a great number of people who are socializing in isolation, who have understood this, and who will now take pleasure in the opportunity to get to know their fellow individuals.

Not until after a few months of utilising social media does one begin to experience the significant effects of using it. This is what they are:

A COMPARISON OF -

When I was buying my automobile, I recall making sure that it was more expensive than one of my relatives' cars, but not necessarily better. The fact that he flaunts his automobile in his Whatsapp status when the family is there is something that I just cannot comprehend. This was a game that I had to win. My actions were the cause of the unwarranted societal pressure that I generated. I responded to that pressure, and when I realized that I had won it, a few months later, another relative of mine purchased a more expensive automobile.

It's possible that he didn't enjoy the fact that I was showing it off to him. Here is how the process works. The picture of the vacation, the expensive restaurants, the clothing, the jewelry, the lifestyles and be choice of books.

There is a secret theory of validation which is very apt and common in social media . I am intending to buy a washing machine . Though I have very limited knowledge of washing machines, still I kind of find a particular machine good . Then I found out one of the celebrities I follow (who may not be an expert in washing machines) uses the same machine . This provides me validation , that I can buy the same items . No logic , no reasoning, just validation .

I socialize with this celebrity , I am sub - consciously following him . This is how this comparison theory works . My grass has to be greener than yours

.

ANXIETY -

The feeling of unrest can be because of anything , someone not doing a work the way you wanted to be done , someone constantly flaunting his lifestyle , some cringe content , some talk show with irrelevant details , anything

Basically you are investing in a product that doesn't have an expiry , moreover the investment will bleed everyday . That's how the anxiety develops .

This product adds a new layer everyday , and at a point you feel you are losing out. Everyone apart from you is moving or active . Basically you are scrolling pictures in your bed at a time when you must be sleeping and this makes you anxious , anxious enough so that you can't sleep properly .

Social anxiety disorder affects crores of Individuals . This is the fear of being judged when you post a picture or post . The kind of comments you receive on your posts . The biggest negative impact of Socializing in isolation is when you actually try to socialize you have thrown yourself in front of the cruel world . The world which is merciless , unapologetic , cruel , rude and a critic by nature . You have actually lost the skill to socialize and when hurt you go back to your isolation stage .

CONVENIENT DISTRACTION

The biggest impact of socializing in isolation is a distraction which is so convenient , so guilt free that it feels like an occupation and a perfect source of entertainment . Occupation which doesn't pay .

Social media platforms push us to over socialize . If you are active on social media and see someone online , you get this unnecessary push from inside to send a hi . And if the other person replies , the conversation continues. This is pretty common .

If someone posts a picture of his baby . You may not find this baby very cute , but you cannot ignore that , because you have the pressure to socialize . If you see and don't like you may sound rude , what if he notices this , what if takes it seriously . You have to like this to maintain your place in that society .

If you have ever done this , you can call yourself an innocent victim of socializing in isolation . Amongst all apps whatsapp has the most amount of people who behave in this manner .

The reason is very obvious , Whatsapp has read receipts . You can remove that in personal chats but not in the group ones . If someone posts about his promotion in a group you are forced to like it and in many cases reply to it , because of two reasons , one the group is small and he will definitely notice and second , in a group the person posting a message can see who has read his message .

These pressures will distract you from your work and will impact your thinking capacity, your creativity and your intelligence.

FOMO plays a vital role in socializing in isolation . You are in your room , completely minding your own business , drowning in your thoughts of which new movie to watch , which car to buy , which team will win in finals and suddenly you receive a message with some random discount offer . Now you have picked the phone to see this , but in this duration when you unlock your phone , your hand automatically types , INS..... Or sometimes it doesn't type. It is already there in recent apps . And then the drama unfolds , with your eyes narrowing , you somehow notice a friend who just visited a random place , eating random food and you see it , you notice it and you take your index finger and without any second thoughts you press your finger slightly on the like button .

Have I told you that Socializing in isolation can very likely dwell you into a deep distraction .

DEEP DISTRACTION

If anything distracts you for a moment it is just distraction , but if something can simply change your thought process and impact your further course of action , and distracts you for days , months and in many cases years also is called Deep Distraction .

Let me explain this with a real life example . I was looking for a flat in Bangalore and had a very limited budget . I started looking for flats and while walking to a society met a person who had a lot of contacts in Bangalore and is actively working as a broker , not only for that society but for many other societies . I had hoped that he would help me find a flat which I am looking for , but even after a month of getting regular recommendations from him , I couldn't find a flat of my choice within my budget .

I dropped the idea and he was also fed up with me for being so uncompromising . After 3 months , I had my salary increment and I finished one of my existing loan also . I was in a position to increase my budget to such an extent that I would have got a really great flat from his recommendation list and at least it will make him feel good about it . At Least he will feel that all his efforts were worth it .

I called him multiple times but there was no response . I dropped him messages too , but he simply ignored me . He was active on whatsapp though . I could get that from his regular status . Guess what was his status for . Contact me if you are looking for a flat in Bangalore ,and with a photo of the best looking flats with their complete details. I replied to his status too , but he didn't reply there either . In one of his status he mentioned a company he is associated with . That company had a page on social media . I tracked it and followed . I dm them also but no reply . I dm both on the company id and his personal ID but absolutely no response at all . Maybe he was the owner of that page . He and his company remained on my friend list , and I looked for other alternatives for a flat and finally got one .

One day I saw his status playing tennis with a friend , whom he mentioned as a national level tennis player . An athletic looking person , had thousands of followers . After spending some time in his profile I became a follower too . This tennis guy used to put three or four status every day . Watching his status developed an interest for me in Tennis (not him , I am straight and this story is about to end) Very soon , I was following more than 10 tennis players who were known to each other and were part of a club . I didn't know anyone personally but I was enjoying it with them . I was one of the live audience when one of them celebrated their birthday . I started developing interest in tennis . I bought a racket and joined a tennis academy close to my place .

Now let me come to this point which I wanted to explain. I was attracted to Tennis but I never enjoyed it and that's why I could never understand it

. After 2 months of desperate attempts , I gave up . I slowly ignored those players' tweets , insta lives and other posts . Slowly I unfollowed or muted almost everyone .

That one was a deep distraction of my life . It ended up nowhere , with no learning , wastage of 2-3 months , some money and many opportunities .

Do you realize what happened to me , where it started , at what point I got trapped . I did too , only after coming out of it . When I was involved in it I was enjoying it and couldn't understand that it was just a distraction , which resulted from my Socializing attempt .It happens everyday with a lot of people . Someone who is following a group of ladies who goes into clubs . Someone who is following a group of college students . This makes you a silent spectator .

See , opening a social media app is like opening a refrigerator when you are not hungry . You might end up munching something .

CHAPTER FIVE

Unnecessary Conversation

How do you feel when you lie to get your work done ?

If you are saying that you have not done that ever , great you have lied again , if you say you have guilt , then you are trying to package your lie with innocence .

We do lie , we all lie about a lot of things . It is fine, it is normal . If you do not lie and to avoid lying you with a straight face say no , then you will be perceived as rude .

So it is an emotional battle within yourself , whether to sound rude or a liar . Both lying and rudeness have different perceptions. Lying to make things better will still be called a lie but you may not be penalized in society's court of law .Delivering a straight NO as a reply can be termed as rude , but maybe this is how this person behaves . He is simple , to the point and doesn't mince his words .

The protection which is very necessary in today's world is to avoid unnecessary conversations .

What is an unnecessary conversation ? Let me tell you .

You are working for a company that makes shirts of an average quality for a mid segment market . You are appointed as a salesman in this company . The niche market for this product is lower middle class who will buy a shirt of price range 500 - 800 bucks . Now you are expected to approach retailers to sell your shirts . The retailers know very well that your shirt is for the mid price segment and so will be the quality for it . Now you know very well about the quality of the shirts and so do the retailers . Your major pitching point will be price negotiation with the retailers . As we all know in that segment pricing plays a major role .

But if your discussion involves quality and you keep explaining about your shirt's quality you are stating facts but it is not necessary . It might cost you the deal . This is what happens when you take part in unnecessary conversations .

You cannot control what you will be listening to but at least you can control what you speak .

Conversations form a very important place in our life . You meet an old friend or colleague and start talking about old times. Is it an unnecessary conversation ? .What do you talk about ? Good stuff only right , non controversial , non hurtful . Discussions that bring a smile on your face .

But do you think there would not have been a single moment of controversy amongst you ? .I don't think so . But still you choose to talk about good stuff . What is the impact ? Your body releases Dopamines . Lot of them make your body healthy and fit . It boosts your mood and makes you feel happy . This cannot be called unnecessary conversations.

Let me give you one more example . You are invited to discuss the economy in a tv debate . You did your preparation well , read all necessary stuff about the economy , its present situation , the way forward , the small ignored stuff which is necessary . And then the debate starts with the question ' Do you think our present prime minister is only wasting time in PR events with zero interest in the economy of nations? The rich are getting richer , the poor are getting poorer and whenever you ask him about it he will blame previous governments . Do you think with such rhetoric he will come back in power in next year's elections ?

If I would have been in your position I would not be able to process this . Maybe you will find it difficult too . You are here to discuss the economy but the conversation very swiftly shifted to politics at the start of the debate . What would you say? Anything you say will make you look like a fool because you don't understand politics . Staying quiet is not an option . If you talk good about the economy you will be labeled as boot licker if you don't may be anti - national and best is if you choose to stay neutral you will be cut in between and the next speaker will be asked to speak . What will you do? You have been asked to be prepared about the economy but you are now asked about politics and when you don't make controversial statements you are ignored .

Now the debate continues and almost all the topics , starting from politics to terrorism , bollywood , nepotism , spirituality , India - Pak relationship is covered , except economy . In the last many years if you look at tv debates , few bollywood movies have been discussed more than the economy . That in my understanding is unnecessary conversation . Not necessary , not required . But still almost all news channels , many youtubers and many social media handles are showing it .

WHY is that?

Very simple reason , people love to see this unnecessary conversation , that makes no sense , that is just controversial in nature but will make no difference in any one's life . If you watch a TV debate you are more likely to create problems around you than you would have resolved . This happens because heated tv debates results in anxiety and will make you sick , if not physically , mentally for sure . You will die inside to speak . In Fact if you are engrossed , you are likely to take a side , you will have your opinion . But ask yourself is it necessary ?

The most common TV debates which happen revolves around politics . The lesser we talk about politics , the better it is . No matter how right you sound , how great your ideas are , you cannot make a politician understand the point . The reason is not because they are unable to , but it is because they don't have the intent to understand .

Debates don't happen only on TV but in our regular life also , with our friends , family members , office colleagues and sometimes random people . In a debate if you have only said and not heard , only informed and not learnt it was a hell lot of unnecessary conversation . Not at all useful .

But we do it very often . Don't we ?

Unnecessary conversation happens a lot on social media too . If you have less than 1000 followers , your comments will be easily ignored , if not you will attract comments . Even if you write simple stuff that today Virat has played amazing , it will make someone write something for you .Do you think only Virat has played , what about the another player ?

The unnecessary conversation has not started yet , as it is just a one way traffic , but if you respond to this with whatever way it will start the conversation . Now let me tell you a very important thing . Not all people jump to react , and in all likeliness trolls are ignored royally these days , but conversation is not always vocal . Even if you are reading a comment and mentally preparing a response to it , then also it is a conversation or in better words unnecessary conversation .

This is a game of snake and ladder. With every comment from your side , you will be like a ladder which will motivate you, it will make you feel empowered , and every reply from a troll will be like a snake which will pull you backwards .

These debates are very common in present day scenario . There are multiple apps and platforms which are designed for debates . This encourages people to discuss on every damn topic possible on earth and speak your heart out . But logic is missing in most of the cases , as the main objective of the person debating is to win this debate . Remember success is overrated . This person is putting all his effort into becoming successful in the debate . He wants to shut others down with whatever skill or data he has

. Even if he is losing at any point he will not give up . He will use all possible tactics to slay others , prove his irrational and unreasonable point . He will not give up . This is a battle for him .

After a point it is just noise and this noise is pollution , which will suffocate you if you continue to be part of it .

Unnecessary conversation is like a dream , and like a dream it does not have a starting point . It just starts from nowhere and you feel yourself in the middle of it .You notice certain behaviors which are unusual . You are not a very active participant but more of an observer where someone else is running the show . Like a dream these conversations are unreal but hypnotizing . It will happen in such a way that you will simply sink in . You will also have your moment to contribute , but though it is your dream , you are simply a participant . This kind of conversation changes it's layer after every few minutes . At some point it will be emotional , at another point it could be intense and at some point it will be comic . These conversations will have zero rhythm and no pattern at all because it doesn't have a purpose , it just flows . These conversations are destructive most of the time as it will be a chaos and all the people involved would only be interested in dumping their views .

The more you be a part of it the more you could feel sorry for yourself after the conversation . But what's the point you have already lost your precious time with this and have distracted yourself just enough to spoil yourself . These kinds of conversations stay inside you and eat you from inside . Yes it eats you . There are cases of people dying after the debate because they couldn't handle the chaos .

Trust me , the moment you see that you are sinking in a conversation where you are just pushing hard to prove a point , get out of it . Because you will never be able to prove your point . The other person will not believe you , he is here to win , For him it is that overrated success which he will celebrate . Please keep yourself out of it .

Conversations sometimes are silent too . Infact in any conversation the verbal part is less than 10 % . This means that almost 90% of the conversation is non - verbal. Your voice , tone and body language all consist of communication . How would you deal with this?

Let me explain this . You are in a restaurant sitting in your table alone enjoying your food , or you are in a cinema hall watching movie , may be in a metro station , or in a coffee place , in a shopping complex , in library , in a religious place , in a school , in a college , in a sports field or any such area where you have crowd around you . Everywhere you are involved in unnecessary conversations.

You may not utter a word, but you are communicating. In a restaurant, you are speaking very slowly . You are conscious; you are using cutlery even though you are not comfortable using them. The curry tastes awkward, but you don't complain; after all, it is a fancy restaurant. You have finally finished your food, but nobody is coming to your table with a bill. You see around and notice a staff but you just pass a smile and softly ask for bill .

You still don't get the bill you pass a smile again and ask again.

With the bill you also receive a feedback form . You can write so many things , taste of curry , delay in getting the bill but you ignore that and write perfect in everything. This is how you are communicating with the restaurant.

There could be many reason behind it , you are too busy to give a feed back or you are too sweet to complain . Busy is fine but sweet ? Really .

First of all you are not complaining it is just feedback and secondly you are not sweet you are ignorant . And the kind of people who have done maximum damage to this world are those who are ignorant and do not provide constructive feedback. What just happened in a restaurant was a conversation between you and the restaurant. An unnecessary, meaningless conversation ,which had smiles , positive feedback , which will live a sour experience with you , which will not let a restaurant improve , which will pass on the same service and taste to its future customers. This conversation was simply not required.

There is a another side too. There could be a possibility a customer would get so offended by this that he will start shouting . He will abuse the staff , raise his voice and sometimes will tell other customers also to leave .

Even this conversation is not helpful because abuse and filth will overshadow meaning and feedback . Nobody will understand your point , but everyone will remember for being abusive .

Is it that difficult to give constructive feedback ?

The same kind of conversation can happen at many places where you are the customer. Like a bank, a movie hall , a hotel , a shopping complex and many more but let me give you a different example .

Most of you would be working in an office or would have attended school or college at some point of time . In an office there is a particular type of employee, the Cry Baby - Not new , most of you are aware of these kind of people . This company is not good , this school is not good , this college will not give placements . No matter where they are they will make the atmosphere toxic with their constant nagging. I know my readers are mature enough to ignore them but haven't we tried convincing them when they complain about the environment. I have done it.One of my colleague constantly complains about the office , hr is shit , promotions are shit , IT is shit , everything is shit shit shit . At one point I gave up and told him why don't you change your company . He had a response to that . I am not getting good offers , the moment I get a good offer I will leave this .

I replied , in that case don't you think , this company is doing a great job paying you with whatever skills you have . He replied to that also saying nobody wants to join this company it is just stuck with me .

Do you see what is happening . The unnecessary conversation has started . Do you know when it started ? The moment I first heard him and started preparing a response for his issues . Even if I choose to avoid him it is a conversation .Leaving the room immediately when he walks in to avoid any of his word enter my ear was almost 55% communication.

You need to learn to ignore ,not avoid . You should not feel his presence . Ignorance is an art and if you don't have it you are a blessing for the society and people around you, who are looking for someone to share their opinions , but unfortunately you are a curse for your own peace. It is a daily practice , you have to ignore the person daily . Slowly you will forget his/her voice and then face and then presence . One fine day you will be working in your work and you will not even notice that he was sitting next to you and talked something .

You have done it already with so many things . Do you notice the road conditions daily , corruption , traffic , the list goes on .

I respect someone who is no-nonsense person, and if you respond to shit , that could still be a meaningful conversation and could make some significant change in your surroundings, but if you simply react to it , then you enter the loop of unnecessary conversation and will impact your peace , health , mental balance and above all it will not make any difference with the problem maker as he will forget his deed and will remember your reaction only .

In this pressure of unnecessary conversation you miss doing necessary conversations . Yes it's true . One of my common observation is that when you indulge in an unnecessary conversation , you miss out many important stuffs . It would have happened with you also . You reach your workplace , with a routine designed in your head and then suddenly you see a mail which is not targeted at you but takes a dig at you . Now your brain starts working . Is it pointed at me .I think so . Let me teach this guy a lesson and you leave all your work and react to the mail . In your anger you are likely to write few things which you don't mean ,but in this impulse driven conversation you are very likely to harm yourself .

On the other hand if your bulb of avoiding unnecessary conversation lightens up , you will not reply to the mail immediately as you have learnt to ignore . You finish your necessary stuffs and then at your leisure period when your creativity is at peak you reply , and now you are not reacting you are responding . This will not harm you , in fact this will not hurt the receiver too , which is definite in the first case . Here receiver will understand your point , because he is most likely expecting your response early morning ,but when the day has almost passed and his receptors are working fine he will see the mail and understand.

Unnecessary lies are very often part of unnecessary conversations. Many of us have a habit of lying , not because of any reason , no intention , no purpose , just lie .Someone asks in your office where were you last weekend and you will say " I was at home" , but the truth is you went out to watch movie with your friend . If he is one of those people whom you want ot avoid then it is fine , and if you are not in mood to talk much then also it is fine because you know it may start another discussion . But it slowly becomes a habit , we start lying just out of no where . In offices you see this behaviour quite often . Because an office is very much like a Big Boss set , with a difference that you can go out at night , so the morning dance and waiting bathrooms is not very common in office . And for cooking and cleaning you have staff . But rest of the things is a lot like Big Boss . Yo know you are competing with everyone , so you have to play your cards right . You are being paid to stay inside and if your popularity drops you are thrown out . Camera are around and watching you all the time so each and every moment of yours is getting noticed and you also receive commands from a voice you don't know . And the best part if no matter how much effort you put , the maximum reward is given to the biggest star , who is not in the room and whose only duty is to judge you .Now in this environment you dont trust anyone so you lie , but when you lie daily it becomes your new reality , it becomes your new sub conscious behaviour . In fact you will start noticing this change inside you . " I could have told him the truth , don't know why I lied "

This happens at many places . You need to work on this . This is one of the most common unnecessary conversation we all go through .

We are not the only one who is communicating , even animals does . The difference is their conversations are emotion driven and are unnecessary most of the times . Make your words count , make your conversations count , be it daily life , debate or an office .

Unreal Love

Love , is it an emotion , an exercise , a feeling , regret , habit , or something else which is still not included in the dictionary .

Tell me if you find anything more complicated than love in this selfish world . And I will tell you that love is the ultimate thing and everything else is stupid .

Till that time bear with me to understand the blackhole of love which starts with hope .

I am in love with my wife . I love my parents , my inlaws , my friends , my brother , my other family members , many of my office employees and many others . I have seen many real life examples of true love so I would be a fool when I saw that love doesn't exist but I will be a bigger fool If I don't tell you that there is huge noise around us in the form of unreal love which definitely doesn't exist . Which has a strong surface but shallow from inside .

This love can be seen , the real love cannot be seen . Let me explain in details .

If you can see the world around you , you will see a lot of stuff which is just a sham . Such as

• A couple walking on streets with their hand in hand .

I have done it myself . Well from my experience I can say it is a moment , when you feel good , you feel comfortable , you are into a moment of peace . It is a feeling of being in a parallel universe where every flower smells like daisies , roads are bright and dust free , the wind flows just enough to not disturb you but to make your eyes blink more than usual , no noise but sound of birds chirping , rustling of leaves and gentle breeze .

This is a dream in itself and in this dream no matter whose hand you are holding you mighy feel the same .In your head you are picturising love , you might be looking at your partners frequently and smiling too . But you are just enjoying a stress free moment and great weather with clean roads (LOL) . This is just an example of unreal love and guess what who all got impacted by it . The people who failed to understand this , those who saw it , those who imagined it and also those who will see similar kind of stuffs in movie . Saying this from a personal experience .

Real love can also be a moment in which you are stuck in jam packed local train or bus and could only see each other from a space made from a folded hand and feel happy . A very frustrating experience , painful , suffocating , smelling , still brings a smile on your face . Well that's how real love looks like . Not the first one

• Intimacy

In all possibilities and specially the shape which world has taken there are very few chances that intimacy could mean real love.

The world is changing so are we and the environment around us . We all are very likely to spend some intimate times with people around us . It could be physical or mental . This happens when you think alike . You have too much to share and discuss. This can happen with anyone . Your office colleague , your friend , someone random whom you met in a coffee shop. Intimacy is healthy , it removes your first layer of personality , which is not real for most of us .

Intimacy is very addictive , it occupies a good part of your brain and even if you are doing something else it will somehow connect you to your partner. It will slowly kill your creative brain cells and will not let you think of anything else . Intimacy usually comes from clear communication , which is very obvious after shedding your first layer of personality. You don't think while talking , you don't mince your words . But this is not love . Love is not restricted till first layer , it penetrates two layers of your personality . In love the form of communication is usually not vocal , it is felt .

Intimacy is fun and may lead to love in future but not necessarily. There are 1-2 or maximum three people in world who could see your inner self which is two layer deep . It's magic . This happens when your thoughts crosses each other without seeking validation . In intimacy , the validation still exists . You don't do things without consent . You may not necessary ask but you do a calculation whether your partner will like it or not . Because your attachment is only one layer deep . You still have not reached there .

In love when you have breached that second layer , consent gets diluted with sensitivity. A simple touch is much more meaningful .

In the phase of intimacy if you remember someone , her face would come to your mind often but when you love someone her voice would come to your mind often .

Intimacy may develop into love but in it's original state it is not love .

Attraction is tough to avoid . You can get attracted to anything you come across . A dog , a pen , a politician , a cricketer , a dress , a car , a movie , a video game , anything and not necessary any single person. You can get attracted to many girls or boys at one time , you can get attracted to books without noticing you have many unread books in your shelf. This is not the real problem , this is human nature , you need to be imperfect and that's what defines you .. Till the time it is attraction , it is fine but the moment it starts becoming an addiction it creates problem. .You need to keep yourself away from this at any cost .

I know dogs are cute but if you spend the entire day with a dog they will no longer be cute . It is important to understand how attraction sometimes take over and literally make holes in every kind of protection.

This is very common in teenager but I have seen multiple examples of a working man or woman simply ignoring important stuffs just because of their attraction cum addiction . Now as you are reading this let me give example of attraction of book .

For many of you the attraction of book would have already become addiction , you see a beautiful cover note , a famous author's book , a beautifully designed book store and a book store that serves coffee . Now it is impossible to stop yourself from entering this book store pick those beautiful books and having a feel of it , in some cases smelling too .

This is pure attraction and when your left hand holds the book and your right hand reaches your mobile phone to take a selfie with it , this attraction has got fame also . But when you open the upi app in your mobile phone and reach the cash counter to purchase this , you have reached addiction phase .

This is critical , you need help at this moment . Your heart beats faster , anxiety is surrounding , a mental calculation triggers inside your brain that how much balance I will be left with be after buying this book . At this very moment take a pause and ask this question to yourself , applying little mathematics. How many unread books you have in shelf . And how much time you usually take to finish a book and by that logic when are you most likely to start this book ? If you have done your calculation right and unbiased the answer would be not in this life time , but I give you the benefit of over optimism and self righteousness. Even then the calculation would come to 2-3 years at least in most of the cases . You can buy this book then .

See I am not saying you should compromise with your desires , infact your desires gives you that extra push to earn and work hard , but you need to understand that is your desire coming in your way of earning and working hard . Is your attraction so deadly that is not letting you concentrate on your work .

Attraction is mostly delusional in nature , it will show few things which does not exist , which is not there which is only your perception. There are very high chances that in your college days you would have been attracted to someone . And the reason could be anything , her (just for reference it could be him also) simplicity, her style , glamor , intelligence , artistic ability , financial background , anything . Now let's say you got attracted to someone for her simplicity . This will create an illusion in your mind that she is a nice girl . It will form a picture of her house , her parents and her lifestyle in your head. This is a state of illusion as the reality might be completely different from this . And we all fell for this mirage , assume it as love .

Attraction is never long lived . It has a reverse time line . The end is decided the day it starts .The fun part if you will not even realise that attraction is over , one fine day when you open her social media page as usual and see her posts , it doesn't make you feel the way it did earlier . Her smile , her pose everything looks fake and you ignore it conveniently. Let me tell you something like this has happened in many relationships including marriage . Do you think everyone understands the game of attraction, no they don't. The lucky ones get over attraction and those who ride on it reaches a commitment stage . A stage of living life together which is based on mere attraction .

This is very common in love marriage and at a point when his/her intelligence , beauty , simplicity , athleticism, feminism , maturity or any other quality doesn't matter at all . Everything which made you fall for your partner is still there but it's impact is no more . At that point you realize that you stretched this relationship on attraction only .

Once the attraction is over it creates a vacuum and then the bigger problem starts . Nature operates in such a way that it will never leave any space for vacuum , so gradually it gets occupied with something worse . It could be alcohol , drugs , adultery , cheating , loneliness . This is a stage where trust issue creeps in . Not with one person but the entire universe . This is worse than break up . Because break up is common , it can be discussed it will get attention , but lack of attraction will not get enough attention also .

This chain of events which makes an attraction an addiction , definitely needs to stop . This is the biggest protection required in today's life .

Glam-Sham

I have seen painted faces pasted on black and white life . Glam is the biggest unreal love . Though you will be aware but still let me take you to a very mysterious territory .

Let me ask you this ?

On a scale of 1-10 how would you rate yourself in terms of look ?

Now get the best make up done , dress as smartly/beautifully as you can , go to the most lighted area of your house and then rate yourself . If your answer remains same then you can still see yourself behind this packaging and if it increases or decreases then it is an issue . If you have not managed to judge yourself properly, it will be very difficult to judge someone else properly , because packaging will eat up all the reality

You can try the reverse too . Rate yourself from 1-10 with make up first and then rate yourself without make up . If it is higher than before than you have attained salvation , if it is less than it is same issue as earlier . Only if it is same than you are on the right track .

Glam is a sham but still people do it , still I would do it specially when I go to a public place , WHY ?

Why make up is not bad , why make up still plays a very important role ?

Make up is never to look more attractive , a silver coating on a sweet is not to make it look attractive , a garnishing on food is not to make it look attractive , the metallic paint on your car is not to make it look attractive . These exercises are done to make it look presentable .There is a difference.

You dress for an event to look presentable , you follow a uniform to gel in , you put on simple dress in a funeral to express grief , you put on swim suit to make sure you can comfortably swim . Dressing up is an art and it depends on the occasion , it could have any purpose , but the moment it's only intention is to draw attention to look attractive then it could have hazardous impact . Dress as per occasion and dress the best you can , neither you should attempt to look attractive just by dress nor someone should judge someone simply basis dress .

Then only you can beat the mystery of glam . Glamour can add weightage , value but it can never add beauty . So before you get blinded by glam , just speak to yourself the person is dressed as per occasion , that's it . It can be louder than the event, or it can be so dull that it falls beneath the charm of the event . But that is still ok , may be that can be judged but that doesn't define your look at any point .

Here is how the process works.Remember layers of human behaviour . Similarly there are layers of look also . A cosmetic work can either enhance the existing layer or can add a completely new layer. If it is adding a new layer altogether then it is not cosmetic it is masquerading .

CHAPTER SEVEN

Psychological Issues

There are things which can be explained , and then there are things which you have to feel . If success , conversation , social media are not enough there is one more stupid stuff which you should protect yourself . It is inside you , flowing swiftly in the wires integrated inside your head. It is random and triggers basis some external condition . It is called psychological issues .I don't want to hurt anyone by calling this a disease so I am calling this a condition ,

The first one is :-

The emotional switch between guilt and cognitive dissonance

This is a very common phenomenon . To explain this further lets break this and understand . You all understand Guilt . You do something which is not right as per your moral code , then the feeling you get is guilt . After this if you convince yourself that what you did was unavoidable due to situation , it is called cognitive dissonance This happens when your thought process and action doesn't match and it creates a feeling of uncomfort inside you . To get over this feeling you try to think of ways to justify this difference .

For example

You have lied to your partner about smoking or drinking or may be worse, cheating. You have done this . Now when you see your partner caring for you , cooking for you . When you see love for yourself in her eyes you will be under guilt it will make you feel awkward , uncomfortable . You will slowly start hating yourself for this.

But the world is not perfect and so is she . She may get mad at you for something , she may overreact, she may do things which might offend you . Then at that moment cognitive dissonance will eat your guilt , justify your cheating . This will paint your thoughts and you stop feeling guilty about your actions .

This is a constant battle and you are always in self judgment mode . This is a common phenomenon and cannot be changed overnight . But the issue with this is , it develops overthinking . In silence , in your own self you keep thinking about your deed with literally two heads talking to each other . One justifying an act and the other one criticizing it .

This impacts decision making too . For a sportsman where quick decisions need to be taken for a doctor , for a stock market investor ,for a scientist , this becomes a huge problem . You need protection from this and the only way out is either let one thought win or ignore this battle , as it might never reach result and will keep coming with new reasoning .

Altruism & Fomo

Another common issue . You might find it hard to believe but this world is filled with selfless people . Yes there are a lot of people and for some it is a reflex system . You can try yourself by faking an accident on the road and you will see a lot of people offering you help . Few will get you up , one will get water for you , one will rub your clothes and another will park your bike on stand . Then there will be a special one who will think the bike is wrongly parked in the road and will try to park it sideways . He in his head is helping you and the traffic system also but it is not easy for him as he doesn't know how to drive , nor is he strong enough to drag your bike . But he still does .He is unable to find a parking place but he still continues . He is probably taking the bike far from the accident spot and you but he is feeling happy with his effort .

Now what has he done ? He is selfless for sure and is trying to help . He is amongst those people who are ready to help people even if it involves their own trouble . But there could be a lot of people who might be suffering from altruism .It could be the person who crossed the road risking his life to buy mineral water , it could also be the person who almost crashes his bike , just to stop and bring him up .

But your guy had two issues at the same time .By the time he saw you , you will already assisted by many people , your bike was parked , you got water and you also were made to sit in the side with people checking if you have hurt yourself anywhere . You somehow missed the action , but you are suffering from altruism and you cannot miss this opportunity to offer help

.Now at this moment FOMO(Fear of missing out) kicks in What will you do , you then see the bike parked in the not so right place . Then you take this opportunity to take this bike in a proper place , troubling yourself ,troubling the traffic and also troubling the guy who had just fallen down as he as to now walk all the way to reach to his bike .

The world will be a great place if no one tries to trouble other , the world will be a much better place if no one tries to unnecessary help others . You can check this with yourself; you might also be suffering from this . If you have it , you need to self introspect , that you are solving the problem or unknowingly creating one .

Confirmation Bias , Prejudice & Generalisation

I love Sachin Tendulkar or I love the batting of Sachin Tendulkar . Are both the statements same or different ?

Let's check . I am a big fan of the cricketer Mr.ABC . Now if I see news of him misbehaving with someone or he is being accused of some crime , I will not be able to digest it . Why ? He is good in cricket , he may not be good in everything .He may be a nice Batsman, he may not be a nice human being . This happens in the court of Law also . A lawyer or a judge may be suffering from a confirmation bias and may not be able to give a fair judgment .

On the other hand if the judge already has a prejudice against someone and if the same person is accused of crime , the confirmation bias may happen again .

A mix of Prejudice and confirmation bias is lethal and it happens with almost all of us .

We have already generalized and have developed a prejudice for lot of things in our country .A religion , a caste , a profession , state , political party , social ideology , dressing sense , eating habit , employment status , social status .... Almost everything attached to us is generalized and if our actions are not aligned to the prejudice then it leads to discomfort . Somehow dots don't get connected . A necklace gets stolen from a house and it was found out that the maid has not stolen it , some family member has done it. We don't know how to react to this .

Or in a traffic collision, the four wheeler driver hit the auto and it was not the auto driver's error . It will be impossible for our brains to digest this knowledge . In a collision between Auto and Car it was the car's error ? How is it even possible?

In a circumstance like this if the automobile driver lies to you that it was an auto driver's error , you would readily believe him . That's confirmation bias , combined with prejudice . It has ruined your intellect . This is one of the main defenses you need in your life .

Self - Schemas and heuristic

In a world where we make decisions every day , how many of them are well thought of or well prepared . Very limited right ? Heuristic approach is adopting a choice or creating an idea only based on your prior experience without much thought or analysis . The result may be favorable or may be not but if the result is not in your favor you are quite likely to assume that if you would have given some thinking about it then the result may have been different .

Heuristic method is based on the world you observe . In this world, it is believed that we come into contact with around 80,000 people on average. This constitutes less than 0.001% of the total population of the planet. Even if every single eight hundred thousand people behave in the same way, your reality is not the truth of the world.

The behavior that occurs when we have a preconceived notion about ourselves, our actions, our nature, or maybe our responses is referred to as self-schema. For instance, you have not had illness very frequently, and you have this self-perception that you only experience illness very infrequently. Consequently, when you get unwell, your self-concept is thrown into disarray, and it is a difficult pill to swallow.

Mix these two together now.

Without a doubt, you would have formed an opinion about a person based on what they said. Suppose there is an elderly person in your community or a security guard at your office who is impolite. It might also be any member of the staff at your place of employment. At this moment, you find yourself in a circumstance in which you want assistance from any of them. This assistance may come in the shape of a smartphone charger, some cash change, or something else entirely. However, the heuristic method that you are using is preventing you from asking them. You make the assumption that they might not assist you or that they might avoid you. You don't like them, and you certainly don't want to take any obligations from them. You don't mind taking on some difficulties, but you are reluctant to accept assistance from others. In the event that you come to the conclusion that you have no other choice, you will naturally seek assistance. When you ask for a smartphone charger, you do it in a very gentle tone and with an expressive face.

Your colleague declines, and the first thing that comes to your thoughts is, "Even if he had, he would not have given." This is the first notion that your mind has. I am familiar with this individual. In spite of the fact that you do not know him, you make assumptions about him. However, while you are lost in your thoughts and searching for someone else, the same person approaches you from behind and says hello. With a sense of astonishment, you turn around and notice that he is holding a charger in his palm. While your mind is still trying to figure out how he obtained it, he says. However, one of my friends did have it. I did not have it. I need to return your phone to him, therefore I would appreciate it if you could give it back to me after you have charged it to the appropriate level.

The astonishment you felt transforms into shock. You have no idea how to respond to this. Didn't he behave in a nasty manner? How was it that he all of a sudden become so kind? Is he trying to make a move on me?

At this point, you are not yet prepared to accept the fact that he is, in fact, a decent person. You are so spoilt by heuristic that you have reached this point.

Not even this is sufficient. You have a self-perception that you are a sociable person and that you are able to initiate a conversation despite having no prior experience. Additionally, your belief will be shattered in the next several days when you encounter that individual once more. Specifically, this is due to the fact that your heuristic behavior is preventing you from comprehending his positive attitude, and your excessive faith in your own self-schema is compelling you to consider other potential explanations.

It is imperative that you comprehend the fact that if you were a sociable person, you would have engaged in conversation with your colleague a great deal earlier rather than later. I would ask that you be extremely critical of your own behavior. You will be able to cease living in a fool's paradise with the aid of this. It is essential that you have a good understanding of who you are. It is much more vital to know oneself than it is to know other people. In order to avoid forming a snap judgment about oneself based on a small number of experiences, you require protection. If you are critical of yourself, you will never develop a self-schema as a result.

Mirroring and Disapproval of Oneself

The act of mirroring is a highly prevalent practice among humans. We are all prone to picking up and imitating certain behaviors of others who are in our immediate vicinity. Whether it be the tone of voice, the eye movement, the body manner, or the utilization of a certain term or phrase, it might be such things. The fact that this is a habit that occurs subconsciously makes it difficult to resist it. We may all have the sensation that there is a word that is just on the verge of being said. The reason for this is that you have unconsciously taken this term with you from another person. You suddenly become aware of yourself talking while tilting your head to the side. This occurs as a result of the fact that one of your senior employees in the workplace speaks in this manner, and you have adopted this behavior.

The act of rejecting oneself is a more advanced type of lacking confidence. When you are lacking confidence, you do not try anything new, which allows you to save some energy and time. On the other hand, when you are experiencing self-rejection, you are not bothered by attempting anything, but you do it with the idea that you will not be able to complete it. This self-rejection is so powerful that it will prevent you from behaving in an appropriate manner, concentrating on your task, and accomplishing anything.

If you are forced to do something and you end up receiving the desired or better than expected outcome, then your lack of confidence will alter over time. This is similar to how confidence will emerge if you are pushed to accomplish anything. Rejection from oneself, on the other hand, is extremely harmful and will not do anything for you. Depression is the most common outcome of self-rejection.

Agarophobia, anhedonia and syntality

The inability to get pleasure from anything that is worthy of pleasure is what is meant by the term "anhedonia."

It is the behavior of a group that is experienced by an individual, and this is what is known as syntality.

A dread of public places known as agarophobia

Going to a strange area with a crowd is the only time you will experience all three of these feelings at the same time. It might be anywhere, including high school, college, the workplace, the playground, or any other location.

Many of us are now suffering from agoraphobia. In this day and age, that is somewhat typical. At least for the first few seconds, we are all agoraphobic; nevertheless, as time goes on and we become accustomed to the circumstances, our anxiety levels begin to decrease.

On the other hand, we also have the ability to judge the syntality of a group. There is a possibility that the nature of a group is loud, but this may not be the case for all of the members. The behavior of a group does not necessarily have to be the same as the conduct of an individual. Therefore, when we spend some time in a group and instead of criticizing a group, when we engage with individuals, our agarophobia gradually disappears, and we also get an understanding of the syntality of the group.

Because of your anhedonia, you are unable to interact with other people even when you are in this position. because you have made the decision to not be joyful. True, that is the case. There are a great number of people who are proud of their anhedonia, and they undoubtedly experience the strain of not being joyful. For someone who takes pride in being anhedonic, there is no way that anything could change; yet, for someone who wants to change this, all they need to do is this one thing. Whenever someone greets you, it is important to respond with a grin. It is finished. Over the course of time, rest will be taken care of for you. It is clear that you do not need to initiate the discussion; all you need to do is respond.

In today's world, anhedonia, syntality, and agoraphobia frequently come together to create a state of isolation in a person. You require some kind of defense against this sensation.

You may avoid experiencing this sensation by participating in or at the very least observing conversations that are real. During interviews, in the real world, at a party, and in society as a whole. Pay attention to person who is speaking. Although you will have the opportunity to have an opinion about the nature or character of that individual at a later time, you are required to begin listening.

Spontaneous Cognition -

The term "spontaneous" refers to a random quality, whereas "cognition" refers to your capacity to think. When thoughts come to your mind out of the blue, this is an example of spontaneous cognition.

It is a relatively widespread practice to engage in spontaneous thought. There is a member of everyone of us. In the past, when we were not distracted by cell phones or television, this was a regular occurrence; however, in recent times, it has taken on a different shape. In today's world, spontaneous cognition is more irrational, less practical, and farther removed from reality. Allow me to provide you with a list of random ideas that a person has in their day-to-day existence. Imagine that the fan were to fall on me. In what ways will I safeguard myself? Which of my two legs will I utilize to do this? At this very now, millions of others are engaging in the very same activity that I am. In order to differentiate myself from others, what should I do differently? Can you tell me about my most recent dream? May I ask how long I will live? I am attempting to recall another acquaintance from school.

There are certain notions that are strange and frightening to consider.

Is there anyone else occupying the bed that I have? There is someone who is standing behind me, right?

In the same context , I shall discuss a club.

A Club for the Thinkers

Are you a member of this club ?

Okay, I should have explained to you what this club is all about. This club has a group of thinkers. You are correct, and you should not consider this to be a collective behavior; rather, it is the individual behavior of each and every person who is a part of this club. All of the people who are members of the thinking club just think. They think when they are getting ready in the morning, while they are preparing food, while they are eating food, while they are taking a bath, while they are relaxing, while they are reading, while they are watching television, while they are chatting to someone, and even while they are viewing reels on social media. They are able to think regardless of the location, the weather, or the time.

Because you are a member of our club, you require protection. There is a widespread problem known as overthinking, and if it is combined with random ideas, it has the potential to be as detrimental as a sickness.

The implementation of a straightforward and uncomplicated method has enabled me to safeguard myself from this. Maintain a record of all the significant things that require me to give them considerable thought. For example, I needed to purchase a refrigerator, organize a vacation to a hill station, search for new possibilities to make money, manage my diet, and gain strength, among other things that were of some significance. Now, if any random notion would cross my mind, and my subconscious would start separating me from the actual world, there comes a moment when you have the realization that you are getting carried away. At that precise instant, I switch my mind to one of the notions that I listed before in this paragraph. In spite of the fact that you invested a significant amount of time and effort on this, it is still an idea that is constructive.

The addition of this safeguard not only provides a new depth to your creative thinking, but it also adds a protection that prevents you from getting sidetracked by thoughts that are completely unpredictable.

Last !!!

Is the first narrative still fresh in your mind?

I will applaud you if you do. I promise you, while I type these following sentences, my right hand is still raising a salute to you.

The inmate had a profound insight into one of the world's most underappreciated theories: the idea that success is overrated. Seeking success in all we do is futile, or maybe we should just stop trying. Sometimes it's more wonderful to have the experience than to have the results. If you had read the article, you would have also learned that the prisoner's discrimination against the outside world is troubling, and that his confirmation bias causes him to lose touch with reality the moment he finds evidence that supports his beliefs. He is in for a very rough ride when he encounters the world.

The jail and his unattainable love will resurface in his memory. He would be enjoying a better life if only he had these safeguards. He needed such safeguards. Some safeguards are required. We don't have few resources anymore; in fact, we have more than enough; the trick is to be selective. The trick is to identify Unreal Love

If I can convince you that these safeguards are essential to your well-being, I will feel my efforts have been worthwhile. .